MAKING MUSIC WITH THE WELLINGTONS A 1960S ROCK'N'ROLL GARAGE BAND

Making Music with The Wellingtons A 1960s Rock'n'Roll Garage Band

Personal

Duane Schultz
3900 N Estabrook Parkway #141
Shorewood, WI 53211
414-699-3612
schultzde8@gmail.com

Making Music With The Wellingtons
A 1960s Rock'n'Roll Garage Band
By Duane Schultz
Approximately 12,300 words

DEDICATION

Making Music with The Wellingtons
A 1960s Rock'n'Roll Garage Band

Is Dedicated to

Dave Rudolph

A lifelong friend, a musical inspiration

and a guy who always had my back

COPYRIGHT

ODE: THE 60S MUSIC SCENE FROM A GARAGE

Blues (3 chord in 7ths, Key of E)
Verse 1
E7
Hmmm. It's early Sunday morning, hardly made it to
my bed,
Say it's early Sunday morning, music's still in my head.
A7
Trailer's parked and tied down. Everything's real tight.
E7
For those musical instruments today is night.
B7 A7 E7 A7 E7 B7
Better get up and go. To my other life
E7
Played a gig up north in Mountain, loaded up at one in
the rain
Thought the dancing would go forever and my voice
would go insane
A7
Here I am smiling and happy. Off to church I go again.
E7
Where I teach those children how to make and to be a
friend
                             B7 A7 E7 C#m7 F#7 B9
That's the life of a teen. 1960s is what I mean
Chorus
A7 E7
Rock and roll is blues. That we know. Three chords in

sevenths here we go A7 E7 B7
E7
Beatles, Stones, Animals, gave us the seeds and we can
plant them as we need
Verse 2
E7
Young people of our little town gather to hear
Their rock-and-roll heroes practice in the rear
A7
Of the town's barbershop where by day Dad shaves a
face
E7
But in the nighttime music fills that space
B7 A7 E7 A7E7 B7
Learn Paul Revere for Friday night is near.
E7
And it's Dewey's tonight, the bar we really love
It's hopping with the hits played on the stage above
A7
Friends around to enjoy the house band tonight
E7
The Wellingtons figured how to play it right
B7 A7 E7 A7 E7 B7
A garage band fit for the time and space.1967 and
done with grace.
Chorus
A7 E7
Rock and roll is blues. That we know. Three chords in
sevenths here we go A7 E7 B7 E7
Beatles, Stones, Animals, gave us the seeds and we can
plant them as we need.

Words and Music by Dean Schultz

ODE TO THE WELLINGTONS

The 60s Wellingtons, what a rock and roll band
Playing that music across the land
Electric guitars and keyboards too
With the drums driving the beat oh so grand
Covering the standards, and singing the blues
For the music, the beat and the dancing too

The teenaged band members staying lean
With energy for adventure and a positive gleam
And keeping that music on the beam
Blending the music with vocals and zest
For the music, the beat and a dancing crest

Playing it right, true with the songs and the call
Playing in schools, the bars and dance hall
Rock and soul, pop and all
Songs of love and the lonely, songs of the rise and fall
For the music, the beat and having a ball

Keeping the rhythms and making them galore
Songs fast and slow, move dancers to the floor
The tunes we all knew, the songs we make soar
Doing it for the dancing, and asking for more
For the music, the beat and the fans to please
Doing it for the dancing of the fans to please
Making music with the Wellingtons, it's a breeze

By the author

TABLE OF CONTENTS

LIST OF GRAPHICS

INTRODUCTION

Making Music with The Wellingtons
A 1960s Rock 'n' Roll Garage Band

This is the saga of a 1960s rock-and-roll band in northeastern Wisconsin. The band was formed sixty years ago, so the vantage point of perspective is both good and bad. Memories fade, and without some sparks, time can diminish the sharp story highlights I would like to use in framing this chronicle. At the same time, despite the passage of time, those brightest feelings still live on in my heart, which assists the narrative as it unfolds.

The story of The Wellingtons is first and foremost about music: a love of listening to and making the music of the times. A group of guys commit to getting a band going and sustaining it with a little musical ability and sheer determination. We made the most of the adventures and opportunities that came our way and busted through obstacles that confronted us. Underneath was the relationship among the band members—critical for the success of the music and The Wellingtons.

In the 1960s, many teenagers wanted to be in a band to cover the music the radio and record industry was pushing. The reality for most groups, however, was pretty grim. Many bands never launched and, if they did play a few gigs, were not able to continue on long enough to become successful. My guess is that most bands in our area lasted between three and six months and then broke up. In some cases, older band personnel (in their twenties) had a difficult time maintaining the same membership for a sustained period. Band life interfered with family, and people needed a regularly scheduled work life to earn a living. Other groups lacked the drive or did not have the cohesiveness or talent to make it work. The Wellingtons

1

was a teenage band looking to make great music and groove inside the tunes of the day. As we were in high school, we had some flexibility to commit to the band and a highly irregular playing schedule. Our band stayed together for more than three years.

A good part of the success of The Wellingtons was the music, the band's willingness to learn new tunes, and a commitment to continually make our music better, complemented by our drive and bravado to go out and find new places to play and promote ourselves across the region. Business managers handled this for many successful groups. The Wellingtons had Dave Rudolph (our lead guitar player) and me. The commitment that Dave and I made was central to our scheduling successes, which increased the variety of places we were able to secure gigs, and then play the jobs with all our heart and soul. Not even a flat tire could stop us.

By the way, what do you do with a flat? Fix it, right? We were fearless and confident in getting the jobs and getting up on stage and playing the tunes of the day without worry or regret.

So this is the tale of The Wellingtons rock-and-roll group from an insider's perspective with a unique view of the band's evolution and the making of the music.

~ 1 ~

BEGINNINGS

I grew up on a farm near Oconto Falls, Wisconsin, so work and play were a central part of my life. Living on a farm meant a lot of work—some good, some bad, and some just awful. I liked the tractors and working in the fields. I hated the dirty, boring chores of working with the animals (cows and then hogs), and I detested making fences and cleaning the manure from the animal pens. *Farming* and *work* were synonymous. There was always more work than time to get it done. A key part of the job was to properly prioritize the projects and take care of those tasks while not ignoring other lesser items on the list. But doing that farm work was a gift. It taught me the patience needed to see projects through to their end and gave me the strength and persistence to overcome the obstacles and set-backs that everyone faces. It toughened me up for life and made me resilient. And it helped me see that hard work brings its own rewards.

Planting crops in the spring gave me the opportunity to drive the tractors while doing the field work: plowing, disking, and sowing the corn or oats. Summer meant baling hay and combining oats and wheat. The sweet smell of freshly cut hay is a wonderful country smell. It stays with your senses and lightens the heart. My father always loved the harvest as a sign of farming success. Rather than buying the newest or the latest farm equipment, he went to the secondhand farm implement market to buy machinery that needed continued repairs from the moment he finalized the purchase, which led to inventing ways to keep stuff working with sweat and tears at a lower cost. However, this was his way to farm without a huge debt and high interest payments at the local lenders.

It also made my brother and me vigilant while we were using the farm machines. We had to be on the lookout for broken parts or functioning failures. Little did I know at the time, but we would use this same approach when organizing The Wellingtons. This type of early warning system worked most of the time. Although I was raised on the farm, I never saw myself becoming a full-time farmer. However, the work ethic, the planning and implementation of tasks, and the ability to use and fix equipment were tailor-made for developing a successful garage band.

When I was not working, I was playing baseball, sometimes solo with my dog, Laddie. I was also into playing Cops and Robbers or Cowboys and Indians with my brother Dean and neighbor Norm. We were always on the same team and used our imagination to deal our enemies pain. This included building hideouts and making traps to trip up the bad guys and defeat the evildoers. I also loved to climb trees. My favorite was a fifty-foot maple tree in our front yard, which provided me a view of the back fields. I was not scared of heights in those days, but I made sure to be safe, as a slip could mean a fall, a broken arm or leg, or worse. We also were into exploring. Our farm had woods and swamps, so we would make paths, encounter mythical monsters, and fight real mosquitoes as we traveled through the woods to seek treasures and find adventures. This fooling around was also a foundation of the patience we needed to connect closely with the other members of the rock-and-roll band—to bond, plan, and chart a way forward.

Two technological tools brought music center stage for me as I reached early adolescence. We bought a record player—a cheap portable that amplified music through a tinny speaker—but it worked, and as this was before stereo records, one speaker was adequate for one to fully hear the recorded music. It played records at three speeds, and my brother and I kept it in our bedroom. We would go to the Ben Franklin store in town and buy knockoff 45s. Once in a while, we'd get a favorite group's album or borrow one from family or friends.

About this time I was also given my own transistor radio. The favorite radio shows in our house played the Top 20 hits. We would always listen to the Johnny Saxe Friday night show out of WBAY Green Bay, and we would tune in to WLS Chicago for the songs moving up on the music charts. It was 1959, and a time of musical change. We now had access to music whenever and wherever. I took that transistor radio everywhere with me: to the garden when hoeing, to the barn when doing chores, and to the fields as we were making or fixing fences.

These experiences exposed me to many forms of the emerging music scene—rock and roll, rhythm and blues, and Motown/doo-wop. Dad loved the Grand Ole Opry. The country music radio show out of Nashville was broadcasted every Saturday evening, and our family would tune in on the radio for the music and the talk. We were regular churchgoers, so the gospel tunes as interpreted by the northern Wisconsin Lutherans were also part of my musical lexicon. Of course at school, Mrs. Nelson led us each week in a singing session of the old-time American folk standards, from "The Little Church in the Vale" to "John Henry." While the school did not have a piano, this didn't stop the group from singing. It was a great experience, and as the school had only about twenty students, our singing bounced off the walls and ceiling of that one-room country school to provide a reverb type of sound. To add to these musical experiences, my parents bought an upright piano (used of course), and I was provided weekly piano lessons by Mrs. Blazek. Music was every day and everywhere. So what was the impetus to start a rock-and-roll band? Several relatives and friends moved me toward the garage band and its music in an unintended way.

First was my aunt Hildegard Wesner. When I was about eleven years old, I was chasing around the house with a broom, pretending to play guitar. When we next visited aunt Hildegard, she went to her bedroom and came out with her acoustic guitar and offered to loan it to me so I could learn some chords and maybe even some songs. What a treasured chance for me. I will always be grateful to her, as this gift started me on a pathway to making music on the guitar.

I quickly realized that learning chords on a guitar was really hard. I spent hour after hour getting the fingering down for chords in the major keys. The minor and seventh chords added increased difficulty, but finally I could accurately finger the chords and strings and shift from chord to chord. I learned some basic folk songs such as "Michael Row the Boat Ashore," "Froggie Went a' Courtin'," and "Baa Baa Black Sheep." This gave me practice and the confidence to listen to any song, hear the chords, and then play along with the record or the musical score.

The other person who had an early influence on me was my cousin Mel Raatz, a musical talent. He could play the piano flawlessly, read complex music, and play from memory. He knew a wide variety of songs, was a skilled transposer, and could improvise as he moved through any song he played. Around this time he also procured a guitar. We listened to one of our favorite groups—the Beach Boys—and practiced the chords and harmonies to their songs, often singing along with their record hits; "In My Room," "Little Surfer Girl," "Don't Worry, Baby," "Little Deuce Coupe," and "Surfing Safari" were our favorites. This was great practice in trying out the harmonies and using lead and backing vocals while playing the chords.

When I moved from the country school to Oconto Falls junior high school, I met a whole new group of classmates. I found myself in classes with more kids than made up the entirety of my previous country schools: Sunny Slope and Beaver Lake. I made great friends, many of whom lived in the city of Oconto Falls, including David Rudolph, who became a fast and close friend. Dave was also musically gifted and played piano, but he wanted to transition to guitar with an eye on learning rock-and-roll tunes. Many days we would get together at his house and listen to music and practice a bit, as well as dream and talk about becoming a famous rock-and-roll band. As new songs moved up the charts, we would target a tune or two, work out the chords and the lyrics, and practice the harmonies. Dave and I knew that if we were to get better, we needed to get rock band gear and practice a bunch. During this time, Dave, my brother Dean, cousin Dale Reichwald, and I would also play music together and sing with an old microphone, outlining a number of possible tunes for a song list.

These sessions provided us an opportunity to practice chords and play and stay on beat as we tried out our voices with songs we liked. It was a valuable way to get grounded playing music as a group. We would also try out harmonies, call and response, and switch from lead vocals to background harmonies. Dale was insistent on putting together an outline of the songs we practiced, and indeed this list became the first rendition of the songs that The Wellingtons would later use for our gigs. He had a small notebook (a promotional gift from one of the corn seed companies), which became the gold standard of songs we knew, songs we wanted to get down, and songs we liked but would never learn.

Our first real performance opportunity came with a school talent show. Dave and I jumped at the chance to play on stage. The talent show was held in the school gym with less-than-ideal acoustics. The microphone echoed across the cavernous space, and we botched chords as we played a forgettable song for those assembled. We didn't win any talent show prizes, but we were astounded and amazed when our classmates applauded us and encouraged us to keep practicing and improving. The musical connection with the audience was amazing. David and I bonded

with no stage fright or fear, and it was an exhilarating experience. What a rush! I guess being bold was as important as being
good. A corollary to this: It's great to play loud, but you need
to play well, too, because any mistakes are magnified by the
volume of the music. The old adage "practice makes perfect" is
also applicable to avoid fumbling chords and lyrics.

This was during the 1963–64 school year—just as we first
heard of the Beatles, a British band that was bringing a new
sound and new songs to the airwaves. We were enthralled. In
fact, one day we tried to call Paul McCartney with a telephone
number we found somewhere. We did get a ring but no answer
and no call back (an early form of telephone scam?). It certainly
indicated what dedicated fans we were. We had even put together a set of questions for him: How do you write an original
song? Where did you get the weird chords for your songs? How
do you and John (Lennon) collaborate in the writing of the music
and the lyrics? What is your favorite key to play and sing in? We
were sure we could connect and get all our questions answered.

Dave and I had great intentions and plans for our band
dreams but limitations on the money front. How could we get
instruments and amplifiers when we couldn't afford them? Our
solution: we hatched the great moneymaking pickle-growing
enterprise idea. We would plant a field of cucumbers and raise
them for sale to the Bond Pickle Company in Oconto. The idea
for the plan was better than making it happen. We worked our
buns off over the summer planting, weeding, and picking on a
plot of land behind the garage on our farm.

As we implemented the plan, we encountered a harsh reality.
Not all the seeds were evenly planted. Hoeing the weeds was

time-consuming and physically straining, and we ruined many of the plants along with the weeds. We finally achieved the harvest, but the picking was also a physical effort. The challenges were many, but the hot sun, the backbreaking work, and the logistics of getting the cucumbers picked every day and to the Bond Pickle factory didn't stop us. We had lots of time together to dream and talk about all the ways that we would be spending our big money. We were fortunate, as the weather cooperated, and the crop came in with so many bags of cucumbers that we almost were done in.

~ 2 ~

EARLY TIMES

In the fall of 1964, my cousin Mel and his buddies—Randy Elbe on drums and Dennis Metz on bass—started a band named the Scarlet Lancers. I don't know how many gigs they played, but to our amazement, they invited Dave and me to join them for several sessions at area dances. This arrangement didn't last long, but it did serve to whet our appetites and further inspired us to organize our own band.

Dave's brother-in-law, John Knott, connected with the Scarlet Lancers in the summer of 1965. They rebranded as J and the Tempests, playing the area with good audience reception. However, by the end of the summer, Mel was off to college, so the band was breaking up and disposing of their equipment. Dave and I leapt at this opportunity. We purchased their Fender amps, a Bassman and a Bandmaster. We also bought their equipment trailer to haul all the band gear we were acquiring. Who would think that so much stuff would be needed for a band? We cobbled together a sound system, wiring up the PA with old amplifier parts and pieces. We added speakers, microphones,

and microphone stands. There were extension cords and ca-
bling, guitar cords, and stage lights, along with the instruments,
amps, drums, and their related accessories. These items filled
that trailer to capacity, and we had great trust that it would
haul our equipment everywhere without fail, and without any
problems. We were unaware of possible unexpected challenges
with that trailer.

Now Dave and I had the guitars, the amps, and the makings
of a group. We practiced several times a week at our farmhouse,
but that didn't last too long. It turned out that the loud sound
and the vibrations from the practices resulted in cracking the
walls and ceiling of the living room. As a garage band, we didn't
practice much in the garage at the farm. We moved our practices
to Dave's dad's barbershop on Main Street in town, so it would
have been more appropriate to call us a barbershop rock band!

A young guy from Stiles, Jake Baenen, had a set of drums and joined our practices. We also contacted Jim Melcher from Pound, who had an organ and some musical talent, convincing him to join the band as well. So the beginning of the band featured Jake on the drums, Jim on the organ, with Dave playing lead and rhythm, and me on bass guitar. Dave and I handled the vocals.

We talked about what we would wear, where we would play, and what songs we would do. We discussed and debated for many an hour on what to name the band. For a time, we used the name the XLs. I don't know how we acquired that moniker or where it came from, but it didn't last long, and we kept casting about for a better name for the group. Finally, we settled on "The Wellingtons." It sounded both British and working class, fitting the front message for our style and sound.

At this same time, we were keen on making the band circuit to the hot spots in the area. We routinely visited venues at Brookside and Kelly Lake as well as a new place at White Potato Lake. As area high schools shifted from sock hops to live music, they also became targets for our attention. We used our contacts to spread the word that we would love to play for the next school dance, and we were eager to break into the bar music circuit. Like investigative journalists, we found the names of the owners or managers of these places. These people not only were our onsite contacts, but they governed the hours and the lighting, signed our contracts, and ensured we were properly paid at the end of the evening.

We reviewed what bands were being booked, as well as their sound and songs. Who were the cover bands from the region, and was their musical capability on par with ours? Some groups were just starting out and had tuning, chording, and vocal issues. Other bands were polished and clearly professional, providing a tight, incredible sound. These groups served as models for us. The key to a great sound was tuning closely, balancing the musical instruments well, and keeping the vocals coming through with consistency and a clear sound.

We also noted other bands' dress, equipment, and style. This gave us hints on how they presented themselves and how they related to their audience. It seemed clear that some bands played for the music and the dancers, while others appeared bored and seemed to be onstage just for the money. From these visits, we gleaned common song standards, the latest popular cover songs, and what the crowds liked. Just as important was how the bands connected with the people dancing to their music. We wanted to project an image that was consistent with our love of the music, creating a great sound and dancing excitement for the audience. We knew it was important to project that joy, the love of music, to the audience by using smiles and positive projections of ourselves when we were onstage. We would use some dance steps now and then but were careful not to compromise the music or the vocals.

We would return to our practices with plans and dreams, but no worries. We might need to perfect the Chuck Berry tunes, an overlooked Beatles song, a Wilson Pickett, or a blues tune or two. We even learned a couple of polkas. For all of our songs, we would listen, pen the lyrics, and get the chords and beat down while filling in the needed harmonies as we practiced. We kept a list of the song lineup so that we included some slow tunes with the upbeat, dancing songs. As such, we never added those half-fast and half-slow songs, because that led to fewer dancers and less enthusiasm on the dance floor.

We were conscious of the importance of adding songs from the top of the charts. Looking back, it turns out we had several on our song list from 1963, five songs from 1964, six from 1965, and seven from 1966. We wanted to keep people dancing to tunes they knew and could sing along with. Our song list stayed close at hand as we played, but we used it only as a reference. As we ended one song, a band member might call out the next one, or we would huddle together to plan the next offering. We tried to be responsive to calls from the audience to help produce the song lineup. At the break, we would review the list to ensure we weren't overlooking any favorites.

~ 3 ~

MAKING THE MUSIC

The first time we played for the entire evening, it was not a great success. The owner/operator of the Green Valley skating rink and dance hall asked us to play for the night and told us we would be paid, but he wouldn't sign a contract. He promised he would be promoting the band and the dance. This sounded like a great deal, and we took the gig, got to the place, set up, and started playing. There were only about ten people there, and we figured that the crowd would be arriving late. But this didn't happen. There is nothing so deflating as playing dance music for so few people.

We had played for several hours when the owner/operator told us we would not receive a fee for the evening but a share of the door receipts. I remember the band made $15, and my share was $3.50. The positive outcome of this experience was that it required us to be flexible, to roll with the punches and the un-expected. It also gave us the opportunity to test out our music and fine-tune playing onstage as a group. We learned a valuable lesson though: always have a contract in place and be sure that the terms are clearly understood and agreed upon by the parties involved.

It was amazing that this first effort did not distress us or derail our journey to garage band success. It just inspired us to try harder, give higher priority to the organizational issues, and keep improving the music. Obstacles and failures didn't mean giving up. Rather, we were reinforced by our progress, and we doubled down on our commitment to succeed.

As we started to play more dates, we had a visit from Hugo Delzer, who introduced himself as the secretary of the County Musicians Union, Local #648. For an annual fee of ten dollars, we received our union cards, contract forms, and several dates to play for union-sponsored events. We were also told that the minimum fee to play four hours would be, without exception, sixty dollars, and we were entitled to a break every hour. We signed up immediately, as this made us legitimate musicians. We were on the way to becoming stars with our instruments, our band members, our songs, and our union cards. Now all we needed were engagements or gigs with someone sponsoring us.

Our first successful gig was at the Bay View Beer Bar on the Bay in Oconto, a rundown bar, family owned and operated by Ma Brainish. She was a loving bartender who could be strict when the situation required it. The horseshoe-shaped bar took up one side of a large room. A pool table and several pinball machines covered the other side of the place. There was a two-bit stage where Ma said she once hired a polka band, but it didn't go so well. We suggested that she hire us, and we would bring in a crowd with our rock-and-roll sound. She was hesitant but agreed to a sixty-dollar contract for one night. For the first gig, she put up posters saying "Live music for the soul." We were excited and gave it our all.

The place was about half full that first evening, and our music attracted dancers. This exceeded Ma's expectations, and we could see satisfaction on her face as we concluded that night of music. She invited us back and scheduled several more dates with us. We used these dates to polish our music and vocals to get the right balance between playing well and playing with precision. We steadily built the crowds—a success for The Wellingtons and Ma.

We needed business cards and promotional posters. Our business cards listed our band as The Wellingtons and proclaimed "Rock and Roll at Its Best." We then had some pictures taken and chose a couple for printing onto large poster paper. We also needed the right look. Would it be dress up or dress down? We decided we could do both. Jake's mom sewed us some blue coats and a set of polka dot shirts so we matched on the set. This was the dressing-up part. The dressed-down look included dark pants or blue jeans, Beatle boots, and dark T-shirts.

We were joined by a business agent who said he would help us get gigs, but his attention was elsewhere, so he was of minimal help. When we signed Jim as our organist, the business agent was also part of the agreement. In the end, we added his name to our business cards but did not list a contact telephone number for him. What is a band's business agent without a way to get in touch? He was an agent without any authority and basically served no role for the band. The only phone numbers on the business cards were Dave's and mine. Dave and I wanted to be in control of the band, its schedule, and its destiny. We were highly protective of our reputation and our image without any animus between us. Dave and I also acted as the advance team for the band, helping to get our schedules organized as the contracts were signed.

These initial gigs led to a number of well-attended dates at area high schools. A return invitation let us know we were successful and our music was appreciated. For the high school gigs, it was almost always girls from a specific extracurricular club, an example being the Pep Club, organizing the dance. We either received a direct call of inquiry or heard about the opportunity through word-of-mouth contacts. We thoroughly enjoyed the school dance gigs. We were treated like royalty, as the organizers and attendees were all so positive. Many local high schools sent invitations for multiple return engagements, and often we were approached at one high school dance with a contact to get another job at another high school. At Oconto Falls High, we used the school's Camera Club as a lever to garner gigs. We tried to fine-tune the old rock-and-roll standards while learning several Top 10 songs every month. Covering those songs moving up the charts kept our playlist current. These ongoing gigs also established our reputation, and we received event-based invitations for picnics and parties. One of the prestigious opportunities was playing for the Oconto Falls paper mill's Christmas party. This was always well attended and gave us the chance to play for our hometown audience.

After about six months of gigs, our organist, Jim, informed us he was leaving the group. He didn't really give us a reason, but I think that the grind and the pace of the band got to him. It's not for everyone. The band members knew that when a gig date came up, they needed to have the flexibility in their personal life to accommodate the band and meet the date. While we only played in the northeastern region, with driving time being for the most part less than an hour, it was also a drain on our teenage bodies, especially if we had back-to-back (Friday/Saturday) gigs.

So we bid Jim adieu. We knew that the band was at a crossroads. Who would we find to fill this keyboard void? Our worries were short-lived, and the problem was solved with our creative energies. Fortunately, we found someone quickly, and the replacement went smoothly.

Brother Dean knew many of the songs on the song list. He, too, took piano lessons and was knowledgeable about the chords, style, and beat of the music we played. When we talked with him about connecting with the band, he saw two hurdles to overcome. As it was still a few months before his fourteenth birthday, he needed Mom and Dad's approval to join the band. Second, he needed a keyboard and amplifier to play as a member of The Wellingtons.

In many ways, the parents' approval was the most challenging. Luckily, I was keeping my grades up and still doing the work on the farm as well as meeting my other family obligations. I'm sure this helped in the negotiations. While we were playing at bars, we were also doing music gigs at area high schools. We emphasized school events as the selling point to encourage our parents' agreement. Most important was the approval and open-mindedness of our folks to say yes, even if it was a hesitant or a temporary yes.

Dean had saved up some money, but our parents had borrowed it for necessary items when times were hard. With their approval for Dean joining the band, they worked to find the money needed to buy him a keyboard and amplifier. We went to Henri's Music in Green Bay and found a Farfisa keyboard and a Vox amplifier. We were able to make a deal with the manager and walked out with the musical equipment Dean needed for the band. With this seamless transition, the band didn't even skip a beat. Dean had a great voice. He took some vocals, and our harmonies improved as well.

About this same time we encountered a third-party interest. Mike Raines was the DJ at the local radio station, WOCO, and he approached us with an oblique offer of assistance. The first time we met, he came walking into the bar where we were playing. My first thought was that maybe he was with the feds. Sharply dressed and smooth talking, he came up and greeted us at break time. He proposed that we meet with him at the radio station after the gig, thinking that would impress us. During the meeting, he tried to gather information about us individually and as the band. Where were we from? Did we write any songs, and what were our plans for the future? He claimed that he could help us a great deal but asked for no money and didn't lay out the ways he could help. We ended the conversation by suggesting that he come to see us at our next gig and we would talk further.

Discussing this among ourselves, we decided that he was angling for the position of recording producer for the group. (Perhaps like Brian Epstein or George Martin with the Beatles, hey!) We did stay in touch with him, as he was a likable guy, but within a couple of months, he took a job at another radio station out of the area, and we never found out what his real interest in our band was.

Mike's replacement at the station was a young man named Chris Lotto, who took up the association with us where Mike left off. We were amazed that these radio guys wanted to connect with us. Chris promoted us for upcoming dates when he was on the air, came to some of our gigs, and was friendly to all of us. Again, if he had plans to become the head of the band, he never disclosed it to us. He never asked for money or proposed any contracts. We concluded that maybe radio guys coming into a new area were just casting around for friends and connections. Perhaps being a DJ at a small radio station was a lonely job and being introduced at a gig and getting a bit of the spotlight and a couple of words with the crowd would help promote the radio station and his programs.

The support of the Musicians Union was great because we got paid for carrying out this grand experiment. For years afterward, people approached our parents or us directly to let us know they attended the Beach Music Fun Fests. My, how they enjoyed those times; they appreciated us as musicians and were grateful to The Wellingtons for playing those outdoor gigs. The Sunday afternoon gigs meant that some weekends the band would play Friday at a school event, Saturday at a bar, and Sunday at the beach. We might as well have been on a road trip!

Our second round of gigs took place at our hometown Dewey's bar, owned and operated by Duward Bohn. The beer bar was located just across the river on the west side of town and was a favorite gathering place for the locals. We approached Dewey and proposed that he should hire us to increase his patronage with some good music; this would be a win for him and for The Wellingtons. The establishment had a bar along one side, with perhaps twenty barstools, a separate area with a pool table, and several pinball machines. In the main area, a corner stage was set about a foot off the floor with room enough for our band. To his credit and our advantage, Dewey signed on to the idea of contracting with us for a night of music. Over the late summer and fall, we played there as often as monthly, and without really having a strategy, we became the house band at Dewey's. Dewey could always depend on garnering a crowd when we performed. There were weekends when we played both Friday and Saturday nights, delighting his customers with our music.

We knew many of the patrons, although we were younger than most in the crowd. We were also confronted with the drunken guys who wanted to get on the stage and become our vocalists. We couldn't tolerate such a challenge, so we engineered a solution: we jimmied together a dud microphone for the "guest singers," and when they protested that they couldn't hear themselves singing, we said that was how the music and vocals blended together, and we couldn't clearly hear ourselves either. We suggested they should just sing louder. We also set the rules, such as no more than one verse or one song or one visit to the stage a night. It was amazing that even the drunk bullies stayed within our rules and were compliant without belligerence.

We rarely found ourselves in threatening or difficult situations with the attendees at our gigs, but we were cautious and aware that sometimes fisticuffs happen because of longstanding rivalries or revenge motivations regarding girls, drinks, or rude statements. I witnessed fights at Brookside and Kelly Lake dances, and common sense dictated keeping a big friend close at hand and having calming words for the bullies who were agitated. Fights in those days were just with fists, or maybe a class ring to mark the opponent's face. I never saw knives or guns in these encounters. Several times at the Tip Top at Anderson Lake, as we were packing up after the gig, we witnessed fights severe enough that the bouncer had to intervene. I was always amazed that given the amount of alcohol consumed by the crowd, we didn't see more fighting—probably because we played a good number of fast tunes, and the patrons were tuckered out from the dancing.

One time after playing at the Green Bay YMCA, we were packing our stuff into the trailer when a group of guys came down the street, looking for a fight. Our car and trailer were parked outside of the YMCA and just across from the district police station, but this location was not a deterrent to the bunch of thugs. As they approached, we said we were ready to be on our way, but they told us they did not like us and planned to teach us a lesson. Now, I knew this wasn't going to be a lesson in manners. The leader of the four or five hauled off and hit me in the forehead with his fist. I had my hand around a microphone stand extension, a steel gooseneck, eight to twelve inches long and about an inch in diameter, so I swung it at the lead thug and hit him in the neck and shoulder area. He and his buddies quickly moved back. Then we saw the cops coming across the street, so we finished loading, jumped in the car, and left town. We laughed on the way home over the fact that the gooseneck had stayed in the same shape as the fellow's shoulder. What had been a scary situation turned into a comedy. The lesson was that a gooseneck at the loading of the trailer is a good defense when necessary.

To help fill our gig calendar, Dave and I would often take a Sunday afternoon to drive across the region and promote our band to owner/operators of potential establishments. We would enter the bar, engage the bartender, and take measure of their interest in hiring a band. We looked for places with posters of upcoming groups, or we would target places where we simply wanted to play a gig. Some places had never had live music, so we attempted to convince the owner or management to consider hiring us on for one or two dates. At times we were successful at this ploy, although often we would fail in our marketing attempts. However, we were never discouraged, as there were always other bars or places to visit and other owners or operators to persuade to hire us.

These scouting trips also provided us leads for other places to target. Several examples illustrate how this worked. We were on the western circuit of the region and heard from an area bar owner about The Cave in Aniwa. We went there to try to get a gig and were successful in getting a contract. We played there one time, but the management was formal and the place just didn't fit us. It was a basement barroom with limited air exchange, a closed space with no windows, and a stuffy atmosphere. So as we wrapped up the night of music, we collectively agreed we wouldn't be returning any time soon.

A second example was Tigerton Dells, described by a bartender at another area bar as nothing but a roadside dive. When we arrived, the bartender and the patrons were friendly and immediately interested in the possibility of a date to play, but they needed the owner's approval. About fifteen minutes after one telephone call, the owner walked in, greeted us, and made us feel great. We signed a contract for an upcoming date. Now this was a real dance hall with ample space for dancing. We were a bit concerned that this would be a repeat of that Green Valley date, but when we arrived for our first gig, we were surprised and pleased at the size of the crowd that showed up for drinking and dancing, and the audience was gracious and affirming of us and our sound. After that gig we were awarded with perhaps six more dates and some wonderful playing adventures.

It is often said that rock-and-roll bands get mixed up in drugs and girls, but the hardest drug we had to contend with was beer. Since our playing took considerable energy, the most we drank was perhaps one or two drinks over the four-hour gig. We often played until closing, and most beer taps were turned off when the music was over. The night was finished for the bar patrons drinking, but not for us. We were our own roadies and had to tear down the set, pack everything up, and load the trailer before catching our breath.

We did have groupies at some gigs—a pack of four or five girls who wanted to flirt with us but nothing more. Again, playing rock-and-roll music was an exhausting exercise for us, and so we were lucky if they blew a kiss in our direction. Maybe they would dance below the stage and applaud or holler encouragement to us. Often, they yelled out requests for songs they wanted us to play or to play again. There were times when the groupies wanted to hang out during setup and teardown just to make small talk, hoping to catch a ride home, or they'd make us small gifts such as earrings or love notes wrapped up with ribbon. None of these encounters were serious or of any consequence, just great fun and ego fulfilling for adolescent rock stars!

We always tried to have a good time though. Oftentimes, when we rolled up to a new location and were unloading to set up, we would talk to each other in a British accent, fooling no one within hearing range. But it was fun and made the time pass more quickly. The personalities of the band members tended toward the upbeat; we didn't have major blowouts or moody, depressive bouts. If we had equipment failures or other screw-up's, we used our collective creative energies to work the issue out and move on past any hurt feelings that might have been involved. We knew that arguing during the performance was not an option. In many ways, we were our own psychologists, as we knew that the music making was reflective of the mood we brought with us. If we were to be successful playing our songs, we required positive energy for the entire gig. We never had to cancel a performance, and we were always ready for adventure. Dean recalls us using a strategy of sitting in the car before unloading at a gig and "fake" arguing and hollering at one another until laughter overtook whatever potential anger or frustration was bugging us. Then we would unload the equipment, set up, and get warmed up to play with light hearts and a great attitude.

The Wellingtons had some favorite places to play. The Tip Top at Anderson Lake was such a place. This place was situated right along side of the highway and just across from the lake. The management staff was positive, and the crowds were great. There was a long bar at the entrance side of the hall, with the dance floor and the stage at the other end. The stage was four feet off the floor, which helped give the place great acoustics. For whatever reason, we could hear our vocals and music clearly, and it made for a much tighter sound. The management generally seemed to appreciate our music, and the location was excellent, as not only did the local kids attend but the out-of-town and out-of-state tourists as well. This resulted in a mixed and different crowd each time we played there. Best yet was that this audience loved to dance, and a majority of the patrons were on the dance floor most of the time. All these ingredients made for great music and multiple play dates for our band.

So why did we cover so many groups and their music but didn't come up with any tunes of our own? This was a time of very creative music making, with well-known groups releasing multiple albums and lesser-known bands doing songwriting and recording. As such, we had lots of choices in our music making and weren't lacking for songs. Also, we did not have the technical capability to record ourselves. The one tape recorder we had access to was deficient, and when we made a tape of our music, we sounded so bad that we burned the tape. And there was our own naiveté. We didn't realize that many hits were just reconstructed renditions of earlier versions, so we assumed we had to write totally original songs. It seemed we couldn't come together on any of our own tunes: Jake was always drumming out some new beats, Dave was focused on new riffs and musical runs, while Dean loved to try out new chord sequences. However, we never were able to get on the same wavelength when trying out an original tune. Because this was not a positive experience, we returned over and over again to covering the songs that others had put out. Perhaps our success in covering well-established songs just got in the way of us writing new music. I can't remember any time when a band member came forward with a song, a fragment, or a song concept. Every time I tried to come up with an original idea for a song, I found that I was plagiarizing something that someone had already done.

What I found great about playing in The Wellingtons was the relationships with the other band members. Our egos were balanced, and competition was not between members but to the standards that any great cover band or bar band strived toward: making the music sound faithful to the recordings of the groups we were covering and ensuring that the tone and beat were always danceable. We progressively improved on our vocals and the harmonies; with some songs we just soared. We had a great song list, and as we became bored or found we had lost some luster for a tune, we moved on to learn a new song that we could pour our hearts and souls into.

We were also fortunate to have a couple of friends of the band accompany us on our out-of-town gigs. Harvey Vanden Bush provided sound engineering and served in the roadie role as well. Always a loyal volunteer, he had great ideas for songs and sounds and assisted us on our trips. We could always rely upon his advice for improving our music and vocals. He had a great ear for how the music came through and would stand in the middle of the dance floor giving us hand signals for the volume and the musical sound mix.

It was on one of those trips across the region that the famous flat-tire incident took place. When we bought the trailer, it came with two original tires, but the deal did not include a spare tire. Now, while we were levelheaded adolescents, we were also knuckleheaded teenagers. We didn't even think about a spare tire until we needed one.

One early morning when returning home from a job, exhausted and getting cranky as the time on the road seemed too long, we heard that awful sound of the flapping of rubber. At

first we thought the car had a flat, but then the chilling realiza-
tion sank in that it was the trailer. And that trailer had no spare
tire. Collectively, we felt sick, as we were just coming to Gillett,
about ten miles from home, with no gas station open at two
o'clock in the morning. After slowly driving through the village,
we spied a gas station that was closed but had a telephone booth.
(This was before cell phones.)

We pulled up near the phone booth, and I grabbed some loose
change and called my dad. I needed help and comfort in that
moment, even if it involved waking the parents in the middle of
the night. Mom finally answered the phone and asked, "Where
are you?" I told her the sad tale of the flat tire, and she said that
Dave's sister had been calling to find out where we might be. By
that time, Dad was awake and took the phone to help solve the
problem. We needed to fix that flat, but how would we accom-
plish it in the middle of the night? Dad's solution was simple:
find an air hose at the gas station. If it was turned on, fill the tire
with air and then drive home. The air hose was outside at the
corner of the building and made a gushing noise when hooked
to the tire valve. We filled the tire with air and went home. The
amazing end to this story was that while we had the tire fixed,
we did not learn any lessons from this. We never invested in a
spare tire. Sometimes learned lessons don't come easy. And the
answer to the question "What do you do with a flat tire?" You
don't fix it; you just fill it with air and then go.

While each of the band members had their own personal life
struggles, we could somehow leave those issues at home. When
we finished setting up for a gig and tuned up and played a
couple of measures, we could just feel the musical voice of the
group coming together. It was getting to that place that made

the musical magic really click. We shifted from four individuals playing four instruments into a single unit that generated amazing rock-and-roll music.

This was true even after we didn't play together for a time. The band broke up after I went to college in the fall of 1967, but we had contracted for several dates the following summer at Dewey's. When summer came, we pulled ourselves together to plan for the gigs. We ran through the song list and learned the Rolling Stones' newly released song, "Jumping Jack Flash." We were rusty as a group and had to practice more than we initially thought we'd have to. It was painful because the layoff was noticeable to us all. However, as we got set up at Dewey's and tuned and played several measures of a couple of songs, we could feel that magic rising from the band. Again, we caught fire in spite of not playing together for about nine months. So these gigs were the last for the band, but we made the most of them knowing that a chapter for us was coming to an end. I think that each of the band members silently committed to do their part in making music with The Wellingtons; not only for these last sessions but across the life of the band.

I am grateful for the experience of playing and making music with a rock-and-roll band from the 1960s. The people, the music, and the adventures served me well throughout my career and helped me to live life with music at the center. My goal was to ensure that my children would be knowledgeable about music, appreciate music, and be comfortable making music. The time with our band also gave me a respect and love of a broad range of music from folk to country to all strands, even soft rap. However, to this day, classical rock and roll of the '60s and '70s remains my favorite.

~ 4 ~

REPLAY

So the formal life of The Wellingtons ended at Dewey's on that last engagement, which was really a summer reunion. Our individual lives went on, with kids and careers and eventually grandkids and retirement. Late in the year 2017, my telephone rang. I picked up and said hello. A gentleman on the line introduced himself by asking if I was Duane of The Wellingtons. This about threw me off my chair. Who was calling and what could this be about? Furthermore, who would be calling for Duane of The Wellingtons? It was Don Moser, who went on to tell me that while The Wellingtons were probably more famous and more musical than his band, The Shadows were better looking.

He was calling with a proposition. Would I consider joining his current band, Jess' Havn' Phun, to host an evening of music themed as a throwback to Dewey's? Now this sounded interesting. We talked about dates and a song list and decided to go forward with the plan. We found some old pictures, and I started practicing the old standards and classics we planned to play. What a nostalgic trip back in time it was! I hadn't played many of the songs we planned for the gig in decades. The words and chords were totally lost in my memory banks. The added irony was that the event was not held at the old Dewey's bar site but at a bar on Main Street.

On the night of the event, we had a decent-sized crowd, including some of my old classmates. We had a practice session to get me up to speed on the songs we were going to play, and I had a great time doing these oldies. Because Don and his band were still playing gigs, they sounded great, and I was mostly a guest in their band. It was good to know that The Wellingtons still lived on in my heart and my mind—and in the hearts of others.

END NOTES / APPENDIX 1

This project was made possible due to the commitments made by The Wellingtons' band members. To Jake Baenen who played drums and to Dave Rudolph on lead, rhythm guitar, and vocals; RIP. In March of 1999, Dave lost his life in a truck accident on a snowy, icy night in the Madison area. Jake died peacefully at his home in 2005. So only Dean and I can still reminisce about The Wellingtons, and I send out my thanks in this effort to Dean as well. I am also grateful to Jim Melcher, who reached out to talk with me about these times and helped sharpen some memories. I assign the memories in this saga to all those who were members of garage bands, knew someone in such a band, or wanted to join such a group. Finally, I devote this story to all music lovers everywhere.

Writing this story took planning, collaboration, and some considerable effort. Thanks so much to my beloved brother who was an inspiration and provided great editorial support. Also thanks to my daughter, Biz, for her encouragement and enthusiasm about this project. Her edits were crucial, as they made the narrative so much more readable. Reba, Deborah and Darya from Ebook Launch did a wonderful job of editing the story and caught many errors that come with any narrative. Any failed memories or errors are on me, and I hope that this project is affirmation to anyone who loves music and wants to make music. For everyone else, I hope it is a way for you to consider making music a more central part of your life, both to ease your pains and expand your joys. A part of the inspiration for doing this project was based on a dream I had back in the spring of 2022, which is included as Appendix 3.

Appendix 1.
Wellington Gigs

Oconto Falls High School

Southwest High School, Green Bay

Marinette High School

De Pere High School

Howard High School

Coleman High School

Green Bay YMCA

Bay View Beer Bar; Oconto

Pulcifer Sportsman Picnic

The Oconto Falls Beach

The Tip Top Club at Anderson Lake

North Beach at Shawano Lake

Gillett, Oconto County Fair

OF Scott Paper Mill Christmas party

The Cave in Aniwa

Lena High School

Pulaski High School

Pulaski Assumption

Preble High School

Green Valley

The Prom

Dewey's

Suring Labor Fest

Tigerton Dells

Brookside

The ShaBon

UW Oshkosh

Memorial Day Parade, Oconto Falls, 1967

APPENDIX 2

The Wellingtons Song List

"8 Days a Week" – 1964, The Beatles

"96 Tears" – 1966, Question Mark and the Mysterians

"All Day and All of the Night" – 1964, Kinks

"All My Loving" – 1964, The Beatles

"Ain't Got Nothing Yet" – 1966, Blues Magoos

"Beer Barrel Polka" – Traditional, 1939 by Will Glahe

"Can't Buy Me Love" – 1964, The Beatles

"Day Tripper" – 1965, The Beatles

"Devil with the Blue Dress/Good Golly Miss Molly" – 1965, Mitch Ryder and the Detroit Wheels

"Do You Want to Dance?" – 1958, Bobby Freeman/ 1965, The Beach Boys

"Double Shot of My Baby's Love" – 1966, Swinging Medallions

"End of the World" – 1963, Skeeter Davis

"Eve of Destruction" – 1965, Barry McGuire

"For Your Love" – 1965, The Yardbirds

"Get Off My Cloud" – 1965, The Rolling Stones

"Gimme Some Lovin" – 1966, Spencer Davis Group

"Gloria" – 1965, Shadows of Night/Van Morrison

"Green Onions" – 1962, Booker T and the MGs

"Hang On Sloopy" – 1965, The McCoys/The Yardbirds

"Hanky Panky" – 1964, Tommy James and the Shondells

"Have You Seen Your Mother, Baby, Standing in The Shadows" – 1966, The Rolling Stones

"House of the Rising Sun" – 1964, The Animals

"Hungry" – 1966, Paul Revere and the Raiders

"I Call Your Name" – 1965, The Beatles

"I Fought the Law" –1964, Bobby Fuller Four

"In Heaven There Is No Beer" –Traditional, 1956,
Ernst Neubach

"Johnny B. Goode" – 1958, Chuck Berry

"Jumping Jack Flash" – 1968, The Rolling Stones

"Kansas City" – 1964, The Beatles

"Keep on Dancing" – 1966, The Gentrys

"Kicks" – 1966, Paul Revere and the Raiders

"Kind of a Drag" – 1967, The Buckinghams

"La Blues" – Unknown

"Land of Ten Thousand Dances" – 1965, Wilson Pickett

"Light My Fire" – 1967, Jim Morrison and the Doors

"Li'l Red Riding Hood" – 1966, Sam the Sham and the Pharaohs

"Long Tall Sally" – 1964, The Beatles

"Louie Louie" – 1964, The Kingsmen

"Lucille" – 1957, Little Richard

"Maybelline" – 1955, Chuck Berry

"Midnight Hour" – 1965, Wilson Pickett

"Money" – 1964, The Beatles

"Mother's Little Helper" – 1966, The Rolling Stones

"Mr. Tambourine Man" – 1965, The Byrds/Bob Dylan

"Mustang Sally" – 1965, Wilson Pickett/Mack Rice

"Nowhere Man" – 1966, The Beatles

"Pretty Woman" – 1964, Roy Orbison

"Psychedelic Reaction" – 1966, Count Five

"Roll Over Beethoven" – 1956, Chuck Berry/1964, The Beatles

"Sergeant Pepper's Lonely Hearts Club Band" – 1967,
The Beatles

"Satisfaction (Can't Get No)"—1965, The Rolling Stones

"Secret Agent Man" – 1964, Johnny Rivers

"Sleep Walk" – 1959, Santo and Johnny

"Tax Man" – 1965, The Beatles

"Ticket to Ride" – 1964, The Beatles

"Time Won't Let Me" – 1965, The Outsiders

"The Last Time" – 1965, The Rolling Stones

"Twist and Shout" – 1964, The Beatles

"Walk Don't Run" – 1960, Ventures/Johnny Smith, 1954

"Walking the Dog" – 1963, Rufus Thomas

"We Got to Get Out of This Place" – 1965, The Animals

"Wild Thing" – 1966, The Troggs
"Wipe Out" – 1963, The Surfaris
"Wooly Bully" – 1964, Sam the Sham and the Pharaohs
"You Make Me Dizzy Miss Lizzy" – 1965, The Beatles
"You Really Got Me" – 1965, The Kinks

APPENDIX 3

The Dream; I'm Just a Promoter of a (Pretend) Rock-and-Roll Band

Have you ever had a dream where you woke up laughing? Well, this was the first time it has happened to me, and I am writing it down so I don't forget it. As you know, I once had a garage band, back in the '60s—The Wellingtons—and we were our own promoters. We would take a Sunday afternoon and drive to various bars and clubs and try to get the owner to sign us up for a gig. We had contract formats, pricing sheets, and a pitch worked out ahead of time. Dave and I did this in Northeast Wisconsin—a radius of sixty to eighty miles around Oconto Falls.

The band broke up when I went to college. Dave got married, Dean joined another group, and Jake went to spend some time in jail. My own life went forward, and except for playing a bit of guitar, I didn't think about a band or doing a gig until several years ago when Don from the old band The Shadows called and enticed me to do a gig with his group. I did it, it was fun, but it was a one-off. Then came this dream ...

I was walking down the street somewhere in Milwaukee when I was approached by a young guy with bleached blond, coiffed hair who was wearing a bright blue suit. I didn't know his name but apparently had met him before because he said, "Are you and the band ready to go on June fifth?" And I replied, "Of course." (This was the first laugh-out-loud moment because June 5 a year later could have been doable, but within ten days?) At the same time, I was trying to recall who this person was. Who did he represent, and what was the gig exactly? I decided he represented the Shorewood Men's Club, which had a summer cookout at the lake.

Then the scene shifted to the mail receiving distribution center in River west. I was standing with Marla, one of my colleagues from the local college and two young people: a guy and a young woman who said she was a singer and could play flute. The guy said he played guitar, and I knew Marla played keyboards. So here was the making of the band I needed for that lakefront engagement. We were standing at the entrance of the building in a garden when this young mail carrier came up with a huge sack of mail, and I asked him if he played drums. He said, "A little, but I don't own any drums." That's when I realized there were so many details that needed to be addressed. The mail carrier/possible drummer (John Prine?) asked about payment, but I don't recall the terms of the contract (if there was one) or the agreed-upon pricing. When would we be playing and for how long? Also on the missing list were the instruments, amps, sound system, and the music. What music would be played?

The scene next moved to Beans and Barley. I was shopping when a local reporter tapped me on the shoulder and asked how the gig went and did the photographer get the pictures. I told him the guy showed up but didn't bring any of his equipment so there were no pictures. Here was another wake-up laugh. He could have just fetched his cell phone from his pocket and then taken some photos.

So that was the dream. If it had any deep meaning, it was lost to me, but it produced some laughs and was vividly stamped into my memory. It also showed me that promoting a gig requires many assumptions with arrangements to be made and agreed upon in advance. I didn't dream about playing the event, so I'm clueless about the music, the band personnel, and the equipment. I also didn't know where it was to be held. The dream did, however, inspire me to give serious thought to write about my experience with The Wellingtons. As I was writing the saga, I realized how complex the various aspects of a band can be. It is about the music, but it's also about the relationships, the scheduling, and the coordination to be the best you can be making music with The Wellingtons.

END

www.ingramcontent.com/pod-product-compliance
Lightning Source LLC
Chambersburg PA
CBHW050231270326
41914CB00033BA/1863/J